Anonymous

1848-1898 - Fifty years of work in the United States of America

Being an account of the entry into the United States of the company now known as

the Liverpool and London and Globe, in the year 1848 and of its work there for fifty

years

Anonymous

1848-1898 - Fifty years of work in the United States of America
Being an account of the entry into the United States of the company now known as the Liverpool and London and Globe, in the year 1848 and of its work there for fifty years

ISBN/EAN: 9783337222130

Printed in Europe, USA, Canada, Australia, Japan

Cover: Foto ©Suzi / pixelio.de

More available books at **www.hansebooks.com**

1848 - 1898

FIFTY YEARS OF WORK

IN THE

UNITED STATES OF AMERICA

BEING AN ACCOUNT OF
THE ENTRY INTO THE UNITED STATES
OF THE COMPANY NOW KNOWN AS

THE LIVERPOOL AND LONDON AND GLOBE

IN THE YEAR 1848 AND OF
ITS WORK THERE FOR FIFTY YEARS;
WITH WHICH IS INCLUDED A BRIEF HISTORY
OF THE ESTABLISHMENT AND
GENERAL OPERATIONS OF THE COMPANY.

NEW YORK, 1898

FIFTY YEARS OF WORK IN THE
UNITED STATES OF AMERICA.

THE Deed of Settlement by which the "Liverpool" was established was duly executed on the 21st day of May, 1836. On the 14th July following an Act of Parliament was passed to carry into effect the objects of the Company in essential particulars.

The earliest proprietors of prominence were Messrs. George Holt, Thomas Booth, Richard Edwards, Thomas Brocklebank, William Dixon, William Earle, Jr., Joseph Christopher Ewart, Ormerod Heyworth, Samuel Taylor Hobson, Joseph Hornby, George Hall Lawrence, Andrew Low, Alexander McGregor, Andrew Melly, James Moon, Lewin Mozley, William Nicol, Charles Stewart

Parker, William Robert Preston, James Powell, and John Ridgway, all of Liverpool. The first Trustees were Sir Thomas Brancker and Messrs. William Brown and Adam Hodgson, also of Liverpool.

The first Secretary (Chief Executive Officer) was Mr. Swinton Boult, by whose exertions mainly the Company was formed, and who later, by his powers of organization, assisted in laying the foundation for that world-wide business which furnishes security at once to the stockholder and the assured against the perils of extensive conflagrations.

The time seemed ripe for the formation of this, the first local company in Liverpool, and the opportunity was offered in a way peculiarly advantageous to the promotion of a varied business in the interests arrayed in the Company's first Board of Direction. Representing every branch of the mercantile community, these gentlemen were in a position in that great shipping centre not merely to influence to the Company a large share of the local business previously distributed amongst insurance companies hailing from other cities, but by their interests

SWINTON BOULT.

HENRY THOMSON.

abroad to acquire important connections for the
Company in the great mercantile centres of the
world.

The situation at this period is well described
in an article relating to the Company, recently
published in the *Insurance Advocate* of Philadelphia,
from which we quote as follows:

DEVELOPMENT OF FOREIGN BUSINESS.

"The city of Liverpool was at this period
rapidly extending its commerce with foreign lands,
advancing steadily toward the position of supremacy
which it finally attained in maritime affairs. Having thoroughly mastered the situation at home, and
seeing in the necessities of those engaged in British
commerce a great opportunity, Mr. Boult inaugu-
rated a policy of foreign extension on a magnificent
and unprecedented scale. He traveled around the
world, establishing branch offices wherever commerce
flourished; applying his trained intelligence and his
practical experience to the varying conditions he
found in different countries, and adapting the prac-

tice of the business to the requirements of each case. Thus, early in its history, the Company took the whole world as its field of operations and became a power in every land where trade had so far developed as to create a demand for the indemnity it had to offer."

Stress is laid on this aspect of the Company's policy in view of the remarkable results which attended the extension of the Company's operations to the United States of America twelve years after its establishment.

The capital of the Company was £2,000,000, of which £66,175 was at once paid up, the design of the proprietors being to rely on the accumulation of heavy reserves to satisfy extraordinary claims for loss, rather than to call up a large capital. That the maintenance of a large reserve was essential to the interests of the proprietors themselves is manifest when the leading features of the Deeds and Acts of Parliament in which the Constitution is embodied are considered.

One of these is that the liability of the stockholders shall not be limited, and that whilst on the transfer of his stock the liability of a proprietor shall cease as between the proprietors, he shall yet be liable on contracts in existence at the time of such transfer for a period of one year thereafter.

This question of protection, alike to the policyholder and the shareholder, appears to have been held steadily in view at all times in the history of the Company, and to this is to be attributed the remarkably large reserves which twice in its history were to afford to each of these interests such complete security that the claim of the policyholder was discharged in full and the stockholder entirely escaped assessment. In this connection, and as justifying this consistent policy of the Directors, the following extract from an early prospectus of the Company is given :

"The Fire Reserves have been created out of the surpluses of prosperous years, and form the best protection possible to both insurer and proprietor, from the effects, not only of the unprofitable years,

In 1846 these had increased to $ 238,815
In 1856   "   "   "   "   1,111,395
In 1866   "   "   "   "   4,090,275
In 1876   "   "   "   "   5,202,945
In 1886   "   "   "   "   6,447,970
In 1896   "   "   "   "   7,764,175

On the 23rd June, 1864, an Act of Parliament was passed confirming the agreement for the amalgamation of the Company with the Globe Insurance Company of London, and changing the name of the consolidated Company to The Liverpool and London and Globe Insurance Company. The Globe Insurance Company had at the time of the amalgamation been in existence for a period of sixty-one years, and the operation by which these two organizations were united has been regarded as one of the most notable events in insurance history.

By this transaction the "Liverpool and London" not merely acquired highly valuable business in London and the provinces, but added to its influential Board of Directors in London the names of

LIVERPOOL.

LONDON.

many gentlemen of prominence in the mercantile
and financial circles of that city.

Not the least of the advantages then secured was
the possession of a choice location in the metropolis
for the transaction of the Company's business.   The
office building so long occupied by the Globe Insurance Company extends from Cornhill round into
Lombard Street, facing on the north the Royal
Exchange and the Bank of England, and on the
west and south the Mansion House.   It is at the
junction of seven streets, and has been often described
as possessing a value per square foot of ground area
not exceeded by that of any other site in the world.

Mr. Augustus Hendriks, now and for many years
the Actuary and Resident Secretary in London, passed
from the service of the "Globe" (which he had
entered in 1852) to that of the consolidated Company.

In 1873—a few years after his advancement to
the position of Managing Director of the Company
—Mr. Swinton Boult retired, Mr. Henry Thomson,
the then Secretary, becoming chief executive officer.

Mr. Thomson had been with the Company at that time nine years. He had been engaged in the service of insurance companies since early youth, having entered the Aberdeen office of the Northern Insurance Company at fourteen years of age. After several changes he became, in 1861, Fire Manager of the Commercial Union Assurance Company, which position he vacated to enter the service of The Liverpool and London and Globe Insurance Company. He died suddenly in 1876 after a singularly vigorous and devoted attention to the Company's affairs. It may be noted that in his reference to the establishment of the Commercial Union above referred to, Mr. Walford in his *Insurance Cyclopedia* says— "The Fire Manager selected by the promoters was Mr. Henry Thomson. It would probably have been found impossible to select anyone better or so well qualified for the task in view."

His successor was Mr. John Matthew Dove, for three years Assistant Secretary, and who became General Manager and Secretary, a position he still holds. Prior to his connection with the Company

JOHN M. DOVE

THOS. I. ALSOP

he had for ten years been in the service of the Royal Insurance Company at its head office in Liverpool as its Assistant Secretary. He was now to exert for the interests he represented those powers which have contributed to the remarkable advancement of the Company, both in the magnitude of its operations and in the results attained. At the sixty-second annual meeting of the stockholders held in Liverpool on the 12th May, 1898, the Chairman of the Company, Mr. Arthur Earle, in moving a resolution of thanks to the officers of the Company, aptly referred to the interesting period in the history of the Company covered by the administration of Mr. Dove in the following words :

"Gentlemen, I now rise to move the following resolution :—' That the thanks of this meeting be given to Mr. Dove (the Manager), Mr. Alsop (the Sub-Manager), and Mr. Hendriks (the Actuary), and the other officers of the Company.' I am sure all here will join in those sentiments. Mr. Dove entered the service of this Company in the year 1873, just twenty-five years ago. The assets of the Company

then were £4,500,000, the fire premiums just over
£1,000,000, and the dividend paid was 10 per cent.,
represented by the modest sum of £25,000. In
1876 he became our Manager. At that time the
assets were £5,500,000, the fire premiums were
under £1,000,000, and the dividend, 30 per cent.,
cost £73,000. We still are fortunate enough to find
Mr. Dove not only as our Manager, but occupying
one of the foremost positions in the insurance world,
our assets now being £10,000,000, our fire premiums
showing an increase of 50 per cent. on what they
were when he first became Manager, and our dividend 90 per cent. representing an annual payment
of £221,000. I think these figures speak for themselves. We are often told 'to judge by results,'
and I cannot help quoting the words of one who
was among the founders of this Company when he
said some forty-five years ago, 'If you only knew
it, you have a gold mine under your feet.' Let us
hope that under the able guidance of Mr. Dove
this may long be the case, and that we may see
him in health and strength on the left of the Chair

BIRMINGHAM, ENGLAND.

BRISTOL, ENGLAND.

LEEDS, ENGLAND

MANCHESTER, ENGLAND.

at our annual meetings for many a year to come. As to Mr. Alsop, his life has been spent in the service of this Company, and he has rendered us invaluable aid in the past as I hope he may also do in the future. Mr. Hendriks in London, will have his hands full this year with his quinquennial, and I hope we may next year be able to congratulate him on the management of that department. The other officers of the Company include, as you are aware, some of the leaders of the insurance world in several parts of the globe. Some are present to-day, but I would ask you to acknowledge the services of all in the resolution before you. Without the engineers the ship cannot steam ahead, and the devotion these excellent officials of yours show on every occasion is above all praise."

Mr. Thomas Israel Alsop entered the chief office in Liverpool in the early sixties, and occupied, in turn, the positions of Cashier, Departmental Chief of the Foreign Department, and Assistant Secretary. He became Sub-manager in succession to Mr. Alexander Duncan, who, after some years of service

with the Company in that capacity, left to undertake
the duties of Manager of the Scottish Union and
National Insurance Company, a position he still
holds.

The home office statement for the year 1897,
as made up in the manner prescribed by such of
the States of the United States as call for it, is
in brief as follows:

Total assets - - -	$56,393,187.28
Total liabilities, including paid up capital -	39,203,497.03
Surplus beyond capital and all other liabilities -	17,189,690.25
Capital actually paid up in cash - - - -	1,228,200.00
Surplus available for policy-holders - - -	$18,417,890.25

Included in assets is the sum of $5,934,091.06,
real estate owned by the Company as in the
Company's books, said real estate being of greater
market value; $8,369,334 in loans on bond and

COMPANY'S OFFICE BUILDINGS.

MEXICO CITY, MEX.

DUBLIN, IRELAND.

SYDNEY, N.S.W.

HAMBURG, GERMANY.

mortgage (first liens), and $33,233,889.18 in stocks and bonds, the par value being $29,971,229.36.

Included in the total given of stocks and bonds is an aggregate value of no less than $7,307,849, representing purchases of bonds of rail-roads and cities in the United States for account of the Home Board, independently of the securities in the possession of the United States Trustees.

As the accounts presented once a year to the stockholders of the Company are in a shape differ-ing from the departmental form above referred to, a table is herewith appended on the American standard showing the Company's condition for the period 1888-1897 inclusive.

Year.	Total Assets.	Total Liabilities excluding Capital.	Surplus available for Policy-holders.	Surplus beyond Cash Capital
1888	$43,535,688	$30,654,347	$12,881,340	$11,653,140
1889	44,982,492	31,488,095	13,494,396	12,266,196
1890	45,814,122	32,547,790	13,266,331	12,038,131
1891	46,822,715	33,991,464	12,831,251	11,603,051
1892	47,260,196	34,189,801	13,070,395	11,842,195
1893	48,254,205	34,750,962	13,503,243	12,275,043
1894	50,728,002	35,431,602	15,296,399	14,068,199
1895	53,049,990	36,531,942	16,517,047	15,289,847
1896	54,716,020	36,904,593	17,811,426	16,583,226
1897	56,393,187	37,975,297	18,417,890	17,189,690

3

At the last annual meeting held in May, 1898, the Directors at the head office of the Company in Liverpool were:

A. Earle, Esq., Chairman,

S. Sandbach Parker, Esq., } Deputy Chairmen,
H. L. Smyth, Esq.,

J. Bibby, Esq.,	Richard Hobson, Esq.,
T. Brocklebank, Esq.,	William F. Moore, Esq.,
Alfred Fletcher, Esq.,	H. H. Nicholson, Esq.,
A. Piggott Fletcher, Esq.,	W. H. Tate, Esq.,
H. B. Gilmour, Esq.,	E. J. Thornewill, Esq.

The Directors in London at the same time were:

Sir C. Nicholson, Bart., D. C. L., Chairman,

G. D. Whatman, Esq., Deputy Chairman,

Sir W. J. R. Cotton,	Hon. S. Carr Glyn,
Charles H. Combe, Esq.,	Right Hon. Lord Lawrence,
F. Fanning, Esq.,	Cosmo Romilly, Esq.,

A. Flower, Esq.

UNITED STATES.

We now turn to the operations of the Company in the United States.

Early in the year 1848, Mr. Alfred Pell of New York was appointed by the Home Office agent for that city and vicinity. In an effort to introduce the Company in this new field, his task was far from easy. Since the year 1812, when the Phœnix Assurance Company of London was compelled to relinquish such agencies as it then had in this country, no European company had entered the United States.

Beyond English houses in New York, or such establishments as possessed English connections, and of such friends and acquaintances as Mr. Pell could influence, we can imagine that the encouragement was small. The Company had been in existence but twelve years, and, as we have seen, its fire premiums in 1846 amounted to but $238,815. It had

no deposits in this country, and the estimate of the
value of its policies when taken had to be formed
upon the representations of Mr. Pell, or of such of
our merchants or bankers as possessed a knowledge
of the standing of the Company. Accordingly, we
find that Mr. Pell in soliciting insurance armed
himself with a certificate, of which a fac-simile is
given below.

The Liverpool and London Insurance Company is well known to us, and in our opinion is entitled to the highest credit. August 1848.

Brown Brothers & Co

Dennistoun Wood & Co

James G. Kingsford

John G. Palmer.

JAMES BROWN

ALFRED PELL. SENIOR.

ALFRED PELL.

The fire premiums on policies issued by Mr. Pell during his agency are as under:

Year 1848 - - - - $ 4,515.
"   1849 - - - -   7,900.
"   1850 - - - - 32,940.

On the 12th December, 1850, by a resolution of the Home Board, a regular branch of the Company was established for the transaction of business in the United States, and a meeting was held on January 6th, 1851 in New York, at the office of Messrs. Brown Brothers & Company, for the purpose of forming a Board of Directors, and for the nomination of Trustees of the funds of the Company in the United States.

It is worthy of note that, even at that very early date, the Company entertained the idea of securing a charter from the State of New York with a view of identifying itself intimately with the land in which it was to secure so large a measure of success. The project, however, fell through.

The following gentlemen, having duly qualified as stockholders, were elected Directors on the New York Board:

George Barclay,	W. S. Wetmore,
James Brown,	Francis Griffin,
M. H. Collett,	C. W. Faber,
Francis Cottenet,	Mortimer Livingston,
Royal Phelps,	E. F. Sanderson.

Mr. James Brown, of the firm of Brown Brothers & Company, was elected Chairman of the Board, and Mr. Francis Cottenet became Deputy Chairman.

The first Trustees were Messrs. Brown and Faber.

Mr. Alfred Pell, having resigned his position as agent, became the Resident Secretary of the Branch and Chief Executive Officer in the United States.

The first agency established was at Charleston, S. C., Mr. James Adger receiving the appointment, and on the 24th February, 1851, an important connection was formed in Philadelphia by the acquisition of the services of Mr. Richard S. Smith, who by his influence and active work quickly established the Company in the estimation of the people of the " Quaker City."

Apparently the agency system prevailed in no important degree at this time, for Fowler in his *History of Insurance*, in referring to the advent of the Company in the State of Pennsylvania, says that a " prestige was given to the agency method " by this event.   He continues : " Richard S. Smith, President of the Union Mutual Insurance Company, was appointed agent for Philadelphia of the Liverpool and London.   This was the first foreign fire insurance agency established in Philadelphia after the exclusion of the Phœnix of London by the Act of March 10th, 1810."

The transaction of perpetual business was at once determined upon, and whilst this feature of fire insurance has been extended but little outside the City of Philadelphia, yet the Company's operations in that branch seem to have been marked with success there from the earliest date of the undertaking.

On the 27th October, 1851, arrangements were concluded with Mr. Charles Briggs to represent the Company at New Orleans.

Mr. Francis Griffin having died, Mr. Alexander Hamilton, Jr., was elected a Director in his place, and was appointed counsel to the Board. (Mr. Hamilton maintained continuously his connection with the Company as Director for thirty-eight years, until his death in December, 1889.)

The headquarters of the Company at this time were at No. 56 Wall Street, an office on the first floor having been leased for the transaction of business.

In June, 1853, Mr. Joshua P. Haven was duly appointed the agent at San Francisco under stringent regulations touching the acceptance of risks.

About the same time it was determined to transact a life business. The plan was put in operation, but a very limited success was realized, and in 1870 all further efforts in that branch were abandoned. Thereafter the time of the Management could be exclusively directed to the fire department, which had already furnished abundant earnest of the remarkable growth later so fully realized.

And now began the connection with the Company of the late Mr. William Warren, who applied for and received the agency at Cleveland, O. He died in harness as Resident Secretary of the Company in Chicago after a long service, alike valuable to the Company and honorable to himself. Later, we shall have occasion to refer to his acts at a very important period of the Company's history.

In pursuance of the policy which had been a marked feature of the Company's operations in Great Britain, as well as in foreign countries, a local Board of Directors was formed in New Orleans, in 1853, following a very promising increase of business in that city.

On the resignation of Mr. Briggs as agent there in March 1854, Mr. Henry V. Ogden was appointed in his stead, and later in the year received the title of Resident Secretary. The first severe loss suffered by the Company in the United States by any one fire occurred at New Orleans at this time, almost the first duty of the new agent being to dispose of claims amounting to about $90,000. Without positive information on the point, it yet seems likely that the rule of the Company providing for prompt payment without discount of

4

claims for fire loss was even then in operation, for the Minutes of the New York Board show that authorization was given Mr. Ogden to draw for the loss "at fifteen and thirty days." As the recorded figures show, this fire served to far more than absorb the surplus realized in three years on the business at that point.

On September 15th, 1854, an agency was established at Baltimore, Mr. Wm. F. Murdoch receiving the appointment, and without entering into other than brief particulars of the opening of connections in other places, it may be said that the Company was represented at this period in the undermentioned important cities:

In Boston, Mass., by Messrs. Edwards & Brewster,
In Savannah, Ga., by Messrs. Bancroft & Bryant,
In New Haven, Conn., by Mr. Charles Robinson,
In Cincinnati, O., by Mr. Howard Matthews,
In Louisville, Ky., by Mr. William Sinton,
In Chicago, Ill., by Mr. John Kinney,
In Indianapolis, Ind., by Mr. F. R. Farnsworth.
Shortly afterwards these were added to by

appointments at Buffalo, N. Y.; Mobile, Ala.; St. Louis, Mo.; Milwaukee, Wis., and other places, and the Company at the close of the year 1854 may be considered as having fully embarked in the agency business of the country.

The minutes of the New York Board at this period show that the Directors were giving much attention to applications for loans on bond and mortgage, indicating that the Company even at that early stage of its history in this country was looking very favorably on this means, amongst others, of investing its surplus funds. The account has shown a steady growth, and stands at the date of this writing (June, 1898) at $3,567,800, a sum, in fact, largely in excess of that invested in this country in like security by any other fire insurance company, native or foreign.

In 1856, the Company instituted a distinct departure in fire underwriting in determining to write railroad property in schedule form. The scheme was put into a practicable shape and received at once the warm approval and support of railroad

officials. The account grew with time and patient
work, and was attended in the earlier years with
highly satisfactory results. After the Chicago and
Boston conflagrations, which served to temporarily
diminish competition, the volume of premiums had
largely increased. With an accession, later, of sundry
companies to the ranks of those engaged in railroad
underwriting, to the consequent steady diminution
in the average rate secured, and to the indisposition
shown by the larger railroad systems to pay premiums in excess of their average losses, is to be
attributed the decline of the business which now
attracts but few insurers, and which furnishes but
scant reward even to such as from their past experience are in a position to discriminate and to
exercise reasonably the power of rejection.

In its agency system in these early days, an
indisposition was evidenced by the Management to
make appointments save in cases where the appli-
cant was willing to represent the Company solely.
This was, and still is, the English system. It was
attended with difficulty in the United States, as

frequently shown in the records of the Board's proceedings. It succeeded in but few instances, and at a later period was, as a policy, finally abandoned.

In Boston it furnished in August, 1856, the cause for a change of agency, Messrs. Edwards & Brewster making way for Mr. G. W. Gordon, who, at the time of the memorable Boston conflagration in 1872, we find in charge of the Company's interests at that place.

In New York City the business was showing a gratifying increase, and different methods than those previously obtaining became necessary. In the earlier years the business procured had been largely on the personal solicitation of Mr. Pell, whose time, however, was now largely devoted to opening new connections in other parts of the country, and in supervising the business flowing in from quarters in which the Company had secured a good foothold. The brokerage system in New York was in its infancy, and insurances were secured either by the direct solicitation of officers or employees of insurance companies, or as a

result of the natural preferences of insurers for
particular offices, often coming through ownership
of the stocks of the companies selected, or by
influences exerted by Directors with their friends
in favor of the companies in which they had an
interest. In this situation Mr. Robert C. Rathbone
was appointed in 1856 a Special Agent for the
Company for New York City, afterwards undertaking
for many years the charge of a branch office
established in Broadway. He deservedly holds the
high position he has earned in the estimation of
his brethren in the business.

The Philadelphia agency was still making good
progress, and, dealing with the year 1857, Fowler
remarks,—"The Philadelphia agency of this Association was taking good part in laying the foundation
of a great and permanent business in the United
States." In 1859 but thirty-three non-State companies were transacting business in Philadelphia,
including four companies of foreign countries, viz :

Liverpool and London,

Royal, (Entered the United States in 1851.)

Northern, (Entered the United States in 1859.)
(Retired in 1862, re-entered in 1881.)

Unity, (Subsequently reinsured by the Liverpool and London.)

It is interesting to note in connection with the introduction of steam engines at fires at Philadelphia, that Mr. Smith was authorized by the Company in February, 1858, to subscribe $250 towards an engine just then built for the Philadelphia Hose Company. Fowler says of this

OLD No.1 ENGINE.
BUILT IN PHILADELPHIA IN 1857 AT A COST OF $3,500.

machine,—"The weight was 7,455 lbs.; time for raising steam from cold water to 60 lbs. pressure, 11 min., 8 sec.; vertical throw of water 120 lbs. pressure and 1¼-inch pipe, 110 feet; with capacity for throwing 306 gallons of water per minute." [1]

Old Print.

A FIRE ENGINE IN 1569

[1] The first experiment in London with the steam fire land-engine in 1829, plunger pump worked direct from piston rod of steam cylinder, did not then lead to the introduction permanently of such apparatus. More satisfactory results were at first attained by the floating steam engine. From 1845 advancing experimentation in construction began in the United States. notably in Cincinnati. In February, 1855, a large steam fire-engine called the Miles Greenwood was brought to Philadelphia for exhibition, and was tested by the Philadelphia Hose Company. The trial indicated that the Miles Greenwood could not throw an equal body of water an equal distance to a good hand engine.—FOWLER.

This subscription can be taken not merely as an early and practical recognition by the Company of the advantages to be secured by the use of the new device, but as a proof of its disposition to identify itself with local enterprise.

On the 23rd April, 1858, Mr. James Hendrick was appointed the agent at Albany, N. Y., thus happily beginning a connection with the Company uninterruptedly maintained to the present and distinguished by a mutual confidence and regard that has been productive of the best results. Mr. Hendrick is hale and hearty, and has held his appointment so long as to be now our senior representative in the eastern agency field. The writer, who knows and values him, trusts that the connection may long be maintained.

In October, 1858, the office accommodation enjoyed since the establishment of the Board in 1851, was found to be inadequate to the Company's needs, and much larger quarters in a new building in Pine Street, possessing a communication with No. 56 Wall Street, were secured.

5

In January, 1860, the building now occupied
by the Company in Cincinnati, Ohio, was purchased
from the Ohio Life & Trust Company.

The question of the personal liability of the
stockholders for the losses of the Company was
presented in an active shape in February, 1860, by
a letter of inquiry from Superintendent Barnes of
the State of New York. The answer was prompt
and unequivocal, and is given below:

NEW YORK, 16 February, 1860.

WILLIAM BARNES, Esq.
    Superintendent.

DEAR SIR:
    In reply to your favor of the 13th inst. All share-
holders of this Company are jointly and individually liable for
each and all of the engagements of the Company.

All Directors must be shareholders. [1]

This liability continues for three years after they may have
sold their interests in the said Company, the purchasers also
being liable. [2]

1 Limited now to Directors in United Kingdom.   2 Now one year.

The following persons, resident in this country, are shareholders:

[HERE FOLLOWS LIST.]

The personal liability of all shareholders of this Company has been so repeatedly stated in our published documents, to which the officers of the Company have sworn as true, and is so clearly set forth and secured in the Deed of Settlement and the Acts of Parliament under which the Company is constituted and empowered, that it seems to us very singular that such an enquiry should now be made.

However, as it is the wish of the Company that this fact should be widely known, and their desire to the utmost of their power to comply with every legal requisition, they readily answer your enquiries, though unaware of the Statute under which such enquiries are authorized.

Yours very respectfully,

(Signed) ALFRED PELL, Resident Secretary.

HENRY GRINNELL, Director.

P. S.—It is this personal liability that leads the Directors for their own protection and that of their fellow stockholders to continue to increase the Company's surplus fund, even though that fund now amounts to more than a Million of Dollars in excess of all the Company's liabilities.

(Signed) ALFRED PELL, Resident Secretary.

As evidencing the readiness to entertain suggestions at this time to prosecute any line of business alleged to offer good chance of success, the Minutes show that the question of burglary insurance received attention. It is presumed that the inquiries made satisfied the Management that that branch of business could not be pursued with profit.

Mr. Joshua P. Haven, having retired from the San Francisco agency, Mr. W. B. Johnston was appointed in his place.

After a continuous service as Chairman of the New York Board since its formation, Mr. James Brown resigned his Directorship in November, 1860, to the great regret of his colleagues and of the Home Board.

In May, 1861, business was suspended in various parts of the South affected by hostilities. Later in the year even the important agency at New Orleans had to be closed, and for nearly twenty years to come the relations which had so satisfactorily existed between the Company and Mr. H. V. Ogden were severed. Later we shall read of his reappointment as Resident Secretary at a time when a large territory had been placed under the supervision of the Southern Department, with headquarters at New Orleans.

The Company had transacted, prior to the outbreak of the civil war, a proportionately large business in the South, and the premium shrinkage was now quite marked.

The United States Branch was a ready purchaser of the U. S. Government securities issued from time to time, and at the close of hostilities held $252,000 of these. This inaugurated the policy of making relatively large investments in Government Bonds. The total has steadily increased, and (in July, 1898,) the market value is $2,198,000.

In April, 1862, the Company made the deposit of $200,000 with the Insurance Department at Albany, N. Y., for the general benefit and protection of policyholders in the United States, as required by law. It had already deposited $100,000 under a law of the same State relating to life business.

The Unity Insurance Company of London was about this time amalgamated with the Liverpool & London, and its business in the United States (it entered in 1857) was turned over to the United States branch of the latter Company.

In December, 1862, the property No. 45 William Street was purchased for use as an office. It may be said at this point that in 1879 the adjoining property on the north was also acquired, being Nos. 47 and 49 William Street, and Nos. 41 and 43 Pine Street, and upon the entire area, (about 6,900 square feet) a new fire-proof eight-story building was erected, which is still the home of the Company and its principal office in the United States. The main office is on the first floor and presents an imposing appearance, the space occupied being exceptionally large. The ceiling is lofty—25 feet high—and floor dimensions of the chamber are 50 by 60 feet. When the building was first occupied it was thought that the space so secured would be ample for the Company's needs, but a large gallery—first tried as an expedient—proving insufficient, the Agency and Accountants Departments were

PRESENT BUILDING.

45-47-49 WILLIAM ST.   41-43 PINE ST.

45 WILLIAM ST.   56 WALL ST.
1862 - 1881.   1848 - 1862.

removed to the second floor, where the floor space occupied is now 2,550 square feet.

The Company had now office buildings at three points in this country, viz., at New York, Cincinnati and San Francisco.

In the same year a severe loss was suffered in the conflagration at Troy, N. Y., the Liverpool & London heading the list of companies affected.

Litigation was now pending between the Company and the Insurance Department of Massachusetts regarding a tax law, the former claiming that as such law related in terms to corporations only, the Liverpool & London, being an "association" was not subject to the tax. The case finally went on appeal to the Supreme Court of the United States, when the decision of the Massachusetts Courts was affirmed. The Company was, for purposes of taxation, held to be a Corporation. The case is interesting and is reported in 10 Wallace 566, under the head of "Liverpool Insurance Company vs. Massachusetts."

Early in 1864 business was resumed in New Orleans under an arrangement with a Mr. Darrow, of a provisional character. In December of that year, Mr. A. Foster Elliott was regularly appointed agent.

On the 4th January, 1865, Mr. Richard S. Smith, having resigned the Philadelphia agency, which he had held with so much advantage to the Company's interests, his son, Mr. Atwood Smith, was appointed in his stead, and he continues to worthily maintain the standing of the Company established in earlier years amidst many difficulties, when the character of its representative was of inestimable advantage in the solicitation of the patronage of the American people.

The firm of Davenport & Company was reappointed agent at Richmond, Virginia, in May, 1865, (and still represents the Company) and this was followed by the reopening of many old connections which had been broken by the war. Accordingly we find that in April, 1866, Messrs. C. T. Lowndes & Company, of Charleston, S. C., received the Company's commission, and whilst some changes have occurred in the membership of the firm, the name itself is unchanged to-day in the list of agents. Two years later a building was purchased for the

COMPANY'S OFFICE BUILDINGS.

PHILADELPHIA, PA.

SAN FRANCISCO, CAL.

CINCINNATI, OHIO.

MONTREAL, CANADA.

Company's use in that city.

In 1867, the Company's premium income had so increased, that it was transacting in the United States a fire business third in order of volume, and was rapidly growing in public estimation.

It may be interesting in this connection to review the figures of the companies having at that time the largest incomes derived from fire premiums, say six companies :

Aetna, . .	$3,310,862
Home, N. Y., .	1,977,031
L. & L. & G., .	1,686,744
Hartford, . .	1,559,040
' Home, Conn., .	1,449,574
' Security, N. Y., .	1,221,920

In August, 1868, Mr. W. Stewart Polk became agent of the Company at Baltimore, Md.

In May, 1869, the Company suffered a serious loss in the death of Mr. Alfred Pell, who had continuously represented its interests as agent and as Chief Executive Officer for twenty-one years; who had borne

---

1 Retired after Chicago conflagration in 1871.

6

the brunt of its many discouragements, and was just then enjoying to the full its remarkable successes. He lived to see the Company firmly established in the United States.

His son, Mr. Alfred Pell, became Chief Executive under the title of Resident Secretary (changed in 1871 to that of Resident Manager) and Mr. James E. Pulsford, who since 1857 had been in the service of the Company at its New York office, became second officer with the title of Assistant Secretary.

In March, 1870, a building was purchased for the Company's use in Montgomery, Ala., so that east, west, and south the policyholders of The Liverpool and London and Globe could note the disposition evinced to place as visible assets easily within the reach of attachment a certain portion of its investments in the United States. This portion at a later date was to be greatly enlarged.

In the twenty years during which the New York Board had been in existence, several changes in Directorships had taken place, and in March, 1871, its membership was as follows:

RICHMOND, VA.

CHARLESTON, S C.

NEW ORLEANS, LA.

NEWARK, N.J.

> Francis Cottenet, Chairman,
>
> Henry Grinnell, Deputy Chairman,
>
> Alexander Hamilton,
>
> R. C. Ferguson,
>
> William F. Cary, Jr.,
>
> Charles H. Marshall.

Mr. Marshall, now (1898) and for many years past the Chairman of the New York Board, became a Director in 1871.

As to volume of premium in the United States, The Liverpool and London and Globe had passed into the second place. It had apparently resorted to no unusual means to accomplish this, if a consideration of its relatively large lines be set aside. Certainly, judged by its expenses, it had furnished no inducement to agents to favor it, as it appears that whilst the average rate of expense of the companies at large had increased in ten years from 27.20 per cent. to 34.35 per cent., the percentage of The Liverpool and London and Globe had been almost stationary (26.53 per cent).

The great test of solvency of the Company

was now near at hand. The Company had received, as we have seen, its baptism in conflagration in New Orleans, La., in 1854, and suffered severely later in Troy, N. Y., and in Portland, Maine. It had for years experienced the penalty of its success in censorious criticism from various quarters, and had been the subject of amusing squibs and comic illustration in an unusual degree. One squib under the name of the "Whirlpool and Undone Insurance Company" dealt with the alleged reckless practice of the Company in the acceptance of large lines. A cartoon largely circulated at the time, pictured the Company as "John Bull" from two points of view. In the front view the figure was clothed in a manner appropriate to the respectability of the character, while viewed from the rear the clothing was in tatters. This cartoon doubtless satisfied the idea of its author that the Company was sailing under false colors, and that confidence could not be placed in its declared resources. So little was the disposition and policy of the Company comprehended by American underwriters of that day that the opinion was freely offered by gentlemen prominent in the business that a serious conflagration would end the career of The Liverpool and London and Globe in the United States. Such a view was founded apparently not upon a doubt of the adequacy of the Company's resources, but probably upon a conviction that in a time of disaster the funds of the United States Branch would not be supplemented by the Home Office reserves.

Quite suddenly the opportunity for judgment came. On the evening of October 8th, 1871, at 10 o'clock at the City of Chicago, began the conflagration which raged fiercely for twenty-eight hours, and which destroyed property covering 2,124 acres. Did space permit, it would be useful as well as interesting to publish an account in detail of this remarkable event, which furnished at once a gigantic and enduring object lesson to the insuring public, and to fire underwriters in every part of the globe.

Advantage has been taken of the concise report of some of the results of this fire appear-

ing in Fowler's *History of Insurance*, and a portion
is here reproduced:

"There was a panic among the insured in suspended non-State companies, excitement and dilemma
among the agencies, and the replacing of the risks
of embarrassed offices in unaffected companies made
a rush and increase of policy writing and record
that taxed the extent of existing and additional
clerical force. The query, *Are* you insured? had a
new emphasis. Non-American companies were high
in public favor. The Liverpool and London and
Globe, next to the Aetna, of Hartford, greatest loser
outside of two swept-away Illinois offices, was an
international insurer not to be affected disastrously
by fire havoc in one locality.

"This conflagration continued for twenty-eight
hours before abating in destructiveness. Rapidity of
combustion was its most marked characteristic, and
it was attended with striking phenomena of evolved
inflammable gases. With the intensity of the heat,
stone disintegrated and crumbled more rapidly than
wood was consumed. It began at 10 P. M. in a

Ruins, Chicago Conflagration, 1871.

cow stable, in the west division of the city, with a strong gale blowing from the south-west, which carried the flame to the north division—a wooden section. The area burned over was 2,124 acres, or nearly three and one-half square miles—seventy-three miles of streets— forming a parallelogram whose width was about one-third its length. The fire was least destructive in the quarter of its origin—the west division. Number of buildings with contents burned was variously enumerated from 13,400 to 25,000, six-tenths in the north division—about nine-tenths of the buildings therein being destroyed (including 600 stores and 100 manufactories), 1,500 acres burned over. Included in the approximately 3,000 buildings destroyed in south division were (lowest estimate) 1,600 stores, twenty-eight hotels, and sixty manufactories. In the west division about 1,000 buildings (lowest estimate) were burned. In the burned district thirty-nine churches were consumed, nearly all the banks, and the most prominent business blocks. Fire Marshall Williams estimated the total loss at $190,526,500,

or $7,621 per building; he placing the number of
buildings destroyed at 25,000. Total loss on buildings
was enumerated by the fire marshall at $52,000,000,
personal property $138,526,500.   Building loss on
business blocks stated as $33,515,000; on brick and
frame dwellings and light business places, $8,808,420,
leaving $9,676,580 to represent the value of all
other real estate destroyed.   Of the total loss on
personal property, $41,000,000 were assigned to
household goods (an average of over $2,000 for each
burned personal occupancy), and to grain and flour
$1,332,500—five destroyed grain elevators contained
1,642,000 bushels of grain. Stocks and business
furniture were counted at $26,775,000; dry goods
(merchandise) $13,500,000; of manufactures—stock,
machinery and products—the value given as lost
was $13,500,000, etc. Of total loss of contents
$58,710,000 were assigned to personal effects, and
$79,816,500 to business property.

"As elsewhere, a fraction of the amount of insurance at risk in the burned district was carried by
non-licensed companies.   According to the excellent

statistical tabulation of the Illinois bureau of insurance, (C. E. Lippincott, auditor of public accounts, William Stadden, compiler of statistics), twenty-two authorized Illinois companies had $34,426,474 at risk in the burned district, 173 companies of other States $59,389,524, and six companies of Great Britain $6,409,782; in all $100,225,780 of insurance in 201 authorized companies. Only $180,208 of the $96,553,721 of losses claimed were resisted. Total capital and net surplus of the 201 companies, according to the official statement of asset values, were $95,214,151. Of the 201 companies, sixty-eight were bankrupted (besides those escaping collapse by the character of their settlements); seventeen Illinois and fifty-one other-state companies insuring about $24,000,000 in the district; the paid-up capital and net surplus of these, as represented, amounted to $24,867,109. By May 31, 1872, it was ascertained that $37,998,986, of the insured loss had been paid (with a salvage and discount on $43,172,747 of loss claimed, of $5,173,761), and it was estimated that $12,106,817 more would be paid, making

7

a total of $50,105,803, or 51.90 per cent. paid of
the aggregate insured loss claimed. It was afterwards estimated that less than $40,000,000 were paid
in all. The six British offices paid 93.08 per cent.
of the claims against them by May 31—more than
one-half being paid by The Liverpool and London
and Globe, *i. e.*, $3,270,780."

Fowler continues: "Chicago had four times
greater fire loss in two days than Philadelphia in
all its history, but in the last three years Philadelphia had burned nearly three millions per annum,
and the conflagration prospects were different from
what had prevailed. Further than this, the signifi-
cance of Chicago was, that no city can insure itself
(or, in other words, city offices writing merely local
risks were predestined failures when the severity of
trial came); and though as yet the agency system
had inadequately brought the concentrated general
security to bear upon each particular point, the insurance economy inculcated the principle of the
widest distribution of loss, and 'bear ye one-
another's burdens' was a sacred injunction."

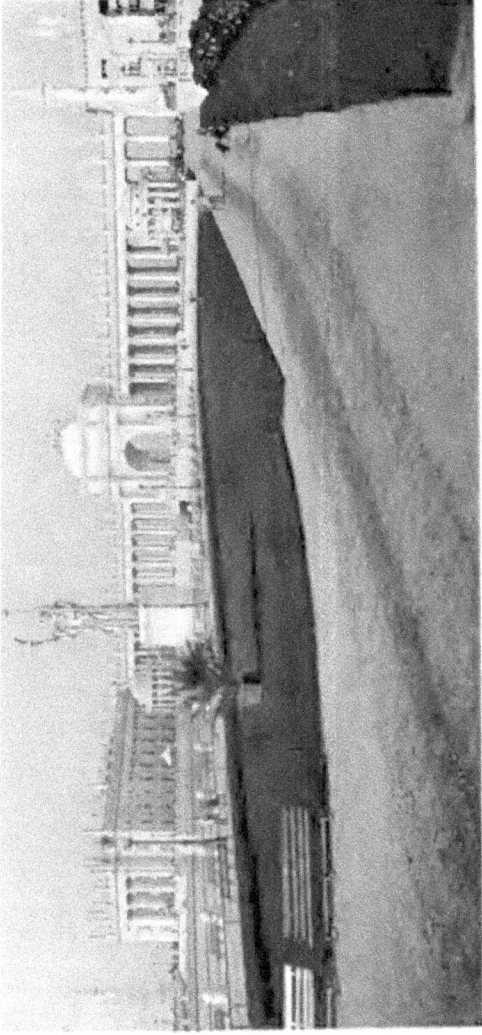

Court of Honor, World's Fair, Chicago, 1893.

Touching the extent to which the Company was involved in this catastrophe, it must not be forgotten that at the time of the occurrence the business it was transacting in the United States was, in volume of premium, second only to that of the Aetna Insurance Company of Hartford, and was largely in excess of that of any foreign company. After twenty-three years of work in America, The Liverpool and London and Globe had fully embarked in the agency business side by side with the great American companies of that day, and under a policy differing in no material degree from that which governed them, and its loss, judged by the volume of its business, bore on the whole no unfavorable comparison with its principal competitors, alike sufferers with it. Large as was this loss, it fell short of the sum total of satisfied claims on the Aetna, a company possessed of an enterprise modified and controlled by the conservatism which has been a prominent feature in its history. [1]

1 Losses reaching $2,000,000 and over [*Argus*]

Aetna of Hartford,	$3,766,423
The Liverpool and London and Globe,	3,270,780
Home, N. Y.,	3,071,390
North British and Mercantile,	2,278,753
Hartford,	2,000,000

Mr. William Warren was now in charge in Chicago as General Agent. After leaving Cleveland, O., he joined Mr. Robert Knight for a time in Cincinnati, O., as Associate General Agent, but for some years prior to the Chicago fire (since 1866) he had a separate field of supervision, reporting to the New York office. It is well to tell the story of the action of this worthy gentleman and accomplished representative in the emergency presented. His son, Mr. William S. Warren, now Resident Secretary of the Chicago Branch of the Company, and himself a spectator of a remarkable scene during the fire, writes of it as follows:

"When the appalling disaster of the 'Great Fire' of Chicago, October 9th, 1871, and the enormous losses, amounting to nearly two hundred millions, had become fully known; among the many thousands who had sustained losses, the responsibilities and the possible payment of claims by the insurance companies having policies involved in this terrible catastrophe was the question of the hour, and many were the inquiries passed among Chicago business men, whose fortunes had apparently been wrecked, as to what proportion of the losses the insurance companies would be able to pay. What amount of all its known millions of loss will The Liverpool and London and Globe Insurance Company pay?

"On the morning of October 10th, and while the fire was still in progress, there was a large gathering of business men of Chicago on the lawn in front of the country home of Mr. William Warren, the General Agent of The Liverpool and London and Globe Insurance Company, at Lake Forest, Ill. Many of these gentlemen representing the leading firms of Chicago had received telegrams from other Chicagoans who had insured all their property in that Company, and whose future was thus largely placed in its keeping.

"While discussing the fire, its limits, and the great loss, Mr. Warren was approached by an elderly gentleman, having a large family solely depending upon him for support, all of whose buildings had been destroyed, and all insured in

The Liverpool and London and Globe Insurance Company. He said, 'All I have left in the world is The Liverpool and London and Globe Insurance Company.' With a face white with intense anxiety and alarm he awaited Mr. Warren's reply, realizing that upon the answer depended his own, as well as the fate of many others. The response was quickly given by the representative of that Company, who said: 'You could not be more safe had you every dollar of the amount of your policies in your pocket at the present time, for The Liverpool and London and Globe Insurance Company will meet all its obligations to the last dollar.' At this reply the revulsion of feeling was too great and the gentleman was completely overcome, as were many of the bystanders. The response was received with heart-felt gratitude, and was taken up by each of the gentlemen present and flashed over the country as quickly as possible to all who were known to be interested. The incident will never be forgotten by those present.

"It is unnecessary to add that the predictions of the payment in full by The Liverpool and London and Globe Insurance Company of all its losses were promptly and honorably fulfilled. The effect of the prompt action of that Company in placing $3,000,000 in cash in New York to pay these losses, besides donating $10,000 to the Chicago sufferers, was of incalculable benefit to Chicago, and the action was fully appreciated by its citizens."

In the meantime the Company's officials in New York were very busy. A special meeting of the Directors was summoned, and a first estimate of loss was cabled to Liverpool as $2,000,000.

The condition of the United States Branch on 31st December, 1870, as reported to the Insurance Department of the State of New York was as follows:

Aggregate assets, - -	$3,054,361.24
Aggregate liabilities, - -	1,588,791.11
Surplus, - - -	$1,465,570.13

To materially reduce this surplus would clearly have been most undesirable, and the United States

Branch confidently expected that the entire estimated loss would be borne by the Home Office.
Nor was it disappointed, for the anxiously expected
response came by cable on the 16th October in
the following words :

"Draw as required up to two million dollars.
If any advantage in bank credit cable us."

The question, then, was solved. The parent
was both willing and able to succor its offspring
to the fullest extent of its needs, and, more than
this, foreseeing the effects of the great enlargement
of its business in the States, was desirous of still
further strengthening during the following year the
funds in the hands of its United States Trustees.

Whilst we find that in the statement of the
United States Branch on 31st December, 1871, as
made to the Insurance Department of the State of
New York, its surplus had in fact been decreased
during the year by over $200,000, it must be
borne in mind that the estimate of loss of $2,000,000
by the Chicago fire grew finally to the large
figures of $3,270,780.

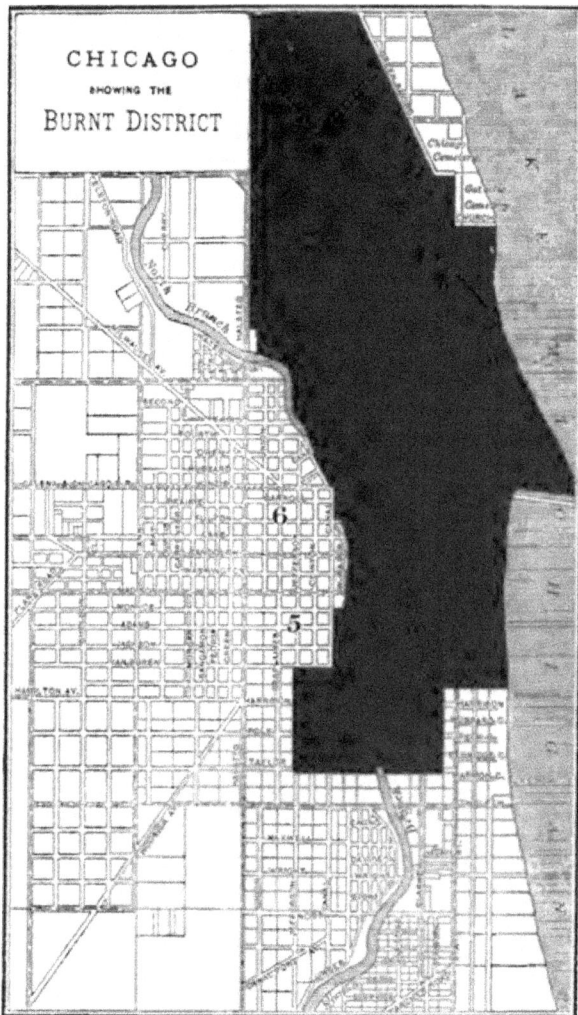

CHICAGO
SHOWING THE
BURNT DISTRICT

8

The effect of the drafts was to reduce the net surplus of the Home Office at December 31st, 1871, to $1,826,638.34.

As if this test of solvency were inadequate, fate was to furnish another and, in one sense, greater ordeal to the Company. On November 9th, 1872, at 7:15 P. M., began the Boston conflagration. This was to affect some companies scarcely touched by the Chicago calamity, notably those hailing from Philadelphia, and to place others, seriously weakened by the earlier fire, in no condition to longer transact business. Fowler reports this fire in the following words:

"The Boston flames were first seen as bursting from the Mansard-roof windows of a five-story granite building on Summer Street, corner of Kingston; the engine-room having ignited, the fire ran up the hoistway of the elevator to the Mansard loft. While the elevator as a flue opening at the top of the building is an escape from the spreading of flame, the elevator closed at top is a passage way for the distribution of flame. An epizootic

prevailing among horses, there was some delay in
bringing the steam fire-engines to the spot, but
for nearly three-quarters of an hour the flames were
confined to the building in which they originated,
owing to the light velocity of the wind, until the
augmenting heat energized the draughts and the
fire was communicated to the window casings on
the opposite side of Summer Street. Then the fire
spread like a fan northward, and after a detour to
the west, further progress ceased at 2 P. M., on
the 10th. Sixty-five acres of a mercantile district
were swept, 776 buildings destroyed, (709 brick or
stone), and in the number were only sixty dwellings. Total firms and business houses burned out,
about 930, one-third of which were shoe and
leather dealers. The real estate was assessed at
a value of $13,591,900, and the structures were
probably worth $20,000,000. Loss on personal
property was estimated at $60,000,000. Aggregate
insurance was about $56,000,000 of which $36,000,000
were in Massachusetts companies. This fire caused
the insolvency of twenty-six Massachusetts com-

panies, whose losses were $30,000,000, with
$16,000,000 of assets.   Four New York companies
and another other-State company also collapsed;
two of the former, the Market and the Washington,
were resuscitations or new incorporations after Chicago
bankruptcy.   Again the foreign companies paid
their losses, (The Liverpool and London and Globe,
and the Royal sustaining more than one-half of
the loss of the foreign companies) and the other-
State companies paid about 95 per cent. of theirs."

JUDY, OR THE LONDON SERIO-COMIC JOURNAL.—NOV. 20, 1872.—(Cartoon reduced.)

"HELP, HELP!"

Once more the Home Office of The Liverpool and London and Globe was called upon for exceptional help, and again it responded without delay and without complaint. The cable message was received on November 11th, and was as follows:

"Draw for loss at Boston as required.

Brocklebank."

The name appended to this comforting message was that of the Chairman of the Home Board, Sir Thomas Brocklebank, who in those stirring times appreciated to the full the exigencies of the situation, and the possibilities of ultimate advantage to the Company.

On the 31st December, 1872, the United States Branch surplus was $1,291,589, an increase during the year of $39,000.

The sums actually paid for losses by the Boston fire aggregated $1,427,729, and if to this we add the total adjusted loss at Chicago, we have a grand aggregate of $4,698,509 disbursed within fifteen months for the relief of policyholders

RUINS, BOSTON CONFLAGRATION. 1872

affected by conflagration, apart from the ordinary
losses of the Company. All of the individual claims
involved in this large sum were paid as adjusted—
there and then, without discount.

Let us note the effect of the calls of the
United States Branch on the parent office.

To stand so severe a strain without impairment
of capital might well excite surprise, and yet by
the sworn statement of the Home Office at 31st
December, 1872, it was seen that the Company
had still a workable net surplus. No stockholder
had been assessed one dollar, nor had any additional stock been placed on the market. For one
year only was the dividend suspended, after which,
beginning with 10 per cent., it has grown without
retrograding, until at the annual meeting of the
stockholders held in May 1898, 90 per cent. was voted.

And if one looks to the fluctuations in the
market price of the stock as a barometer of the
confidence of the investing public in the resources
and management of the Company in this trying
emergency, one fails to find evidences that assess-

large native institutions, and by companies possessing such strong local influences as would ensure
the exercise of a choice of risks. All this was
now to be changed. The Liverpool and London and
Globe took its position amongst the great companies
of the land.

Hardly less satisfactory were the new relations
established with American companies. Viewed before
as an intruder, its position in a time of calamity
uncertain, and known as an aggressive competitor,
respect and confidence now took the place of dislike
and distrust, and the Company henceforth acquired
an influence in the councils of insurance throughout the United States.

The large expansion of business following an
increase in the prestige of the Company induced a change to the Departmental system in the
supervision of business, and in September 1875,
Departments were established, with local Boards of
Directors, in San Francisco, Chicago and New
Orleans, Messrs. W. B. Johnston, William Warren,
and A. Foster Elliott becoming respectively the

HENRY W. EATON.

GEO. W. HOYT.

JOHN J. MARTIN.

Resident Secretaries, reporting direct to the Home Office. New York remained, as before, the principal office in the United States, with Mr. Alfred Pell as Resident Manager, Mr. J. E. Pulsford as Resident Secretary, and Mr. Arthur Pell as Assistant Secretary.

On the retirement of Mr. Pell in 1876 to assume the position of manager of the Commercial Union Assurance Company, Mr. Pulsford became Resident Manager, Mr. Arthur Pell, Deputy Manager, and Mr. Charles Sewall, Assistant Deputy Manager.

The Directors in New York at this date were:

> Robert B. Minturn, Chairman,
> Charles H. Marshall,
> Alexander Hamilton,
> William F. Cary, Jr.,
> Anson Phelps Stokes.

In 1878, Mr. Charles Sewall having accepted the position of assistant manager under Mr. Pell of the United States branch of the "Commercial Union," and Mr. Arthur Pell having retired from active business, Mr. Henry W. Eaton, who had entered the service of the Company in 1866 at the Home Office in Liverpool, and who became in 1876 Resident Secretary of the West of England Branch, was selected for the position of Deputy Manager. Mr. George W. Hoyt, who entered the New York Office in 1871, became Assistant Deputy Manager.

The United States premiums of the Company for the year 1879 amounted to $2,595,521. A reaction had set in from the large rates (we may say emergency rates) following the conflagration period, and now scarcely a local Board in the country remained in existence. The results for some time to come to the companies at large were very unsatisfactory. The Insurance Superintendent of the State of New York ascertained the net loss of the companies reporting to his department for this year to have been $5,854,997.

Towards the close of 1879, Mr. Robert Knight of Cincinnati retired, Mr. James M. De Camp receiving the appointment as General Agent under the New York office for the States of Ohio, Indiana,

HENRY V. OGDEN.

CLARENCE F. LOW.

J. G. PEPPER.

Kentucky, Tennessee and Arkansas, a position he still holds. Mr. De Camp had already served the Company for many years in the capacity of Special Agent in New England.

Mr. A. Foster Elliott of New Orleans, died in April, 1879, and was succeeded by the Company's old acquaintance Henry V. Ogden, who remained in charge of the New Orleans Department until relieved by the Company in 1896 under a retiring allowance, having served in all about twenty-five years. He is spending the evening of his days at Milwaukee, Wis., and any reader of these pages visiting that city will be repaid by calling upon him. The only introduction needful will be a statement that the visitor is a friend of the Company.

Mr. Ogden's successor as Resident Secretary was Mr. Clarence F. Low, for many years Assistant Secretary of the New Orleans Branch. Mr. Low is still in charge of that department. The present Assistant Secretary is Mr. J. G. Pepper, who received his appointment after many years of service as third officer. The territory under the charge of the New Orleans Centre is as follows: Louisiana, Mississippi, Alabama, Georgia, Florida and Texas.

In San Francisco in November 1879, the Company had to lament the sudden decease, as the result of an accident, of Mr. Wm. B. Johnston whose place was filled by Mr. George Mel until August 1881. He was succeeded by Mr. C. D. Haven, the present incumbent of the position, who had had long experience as an officer of a local company in San Francisco. To all who are acquainted with insurance matters on the Pacific Coast, the name of Mr. Haven will be extremely familiar. His assistant is Mr. C. Mason Kinne, who is an old servant of the Company. The territory covered by the San Francisco Branch is as follows: California, Nevada, Oregon, Washington, Arizona, Idaho and Alaska.

Mr. William Warren of Chicago lived for many years following the stirring events in which he played so important a part, and in which, as we have seen, his standing in the community was such that his simple word, at a time when old institu-

CHAS. D. HAVEN.

C. MASON KINNE.

tions were crumbling away, served to effectually allay the apprehension of his fellow-citizens touching the ability and disposition of the Company to satisfy its contracts. He had been closely identified with the early up-hill work of the Company both as Agent and Manager, and survived to see the institution he so faithfully served attain a high position in the country.

Mr. William S. Warren succeeded Mr. William Warren in November, 1889, sharing with Mr. George Crooke the responsibility of management until the retirement of the latter in 1892. Mr. Warren's entire business life has been passed in the service of the Company. He has as assistants Messrs. George H. Moore and John V. Thomas. Mr. Moore became connected with The Liverpool and London and Globe in 1882 as State Agent for Michigan, and January 1st, 1893, was appointed Assistant Resident Secretary. Mr. Thomas was commissioned local Agent of the Company on June 4th, 1874; October 15th, 1881, he received the appointment of Special Agent, and one year later that of State Agent for Illinois until called to his present position January 1st, 1893. The territory under the supervision of the Chicago office is as follows: Illinois, Michigan, Iowa, Wisconsin, Minnesota, Missouri, Kansas, Nebraska, Colorado, Dakota, Montana, Utah, Wyoming and New Mexico.

By the second great fire in Boston occurring in 1889, the Company was relatively not a large loser, but it disbursed its full share in that year at Lynn, Mass., and other places unfavorably affected by conflagrations, the result of these exceptional demands, added to ordinary claims on the United States business, entailing a loss for the twelve months ending December 31st of $164,564.

The account for that year stands as follows:

Fire premiums, . . .		$4,273,371
Total expenditure,	$4,102,971	
Increase of liability,	334,964	4,437,935
Loss, . . .		$ 164,564

Mr. James E. Pulsford, after over thirty years of service, retired in June 1887, receiving as a

THE LATE WM. WARREN.

WM. S. WARREN.

GEO. H. MOORE.

JOHN V. THOMAS.

mark of the Company's appreciation an election to a place in the New York Board of Direction, and the grant of an annuity during his lifetime. He is now eighty-two years of age, is singularly vigorous for a man of his years, and the Company still enjoys the benefit of that good judgment which for so long a time was exercised in his official capacity to its advantage. His photograph copied on another page represents him at eighty years of age and is an excellent likeness.

Mr. Henry W. Eaton became Resident Manager, and Mr. George W. Hoyt, Deputy Manager, positions they still occupy. Mr. John J. Martin was more recently constituted third officer, with the title of Agency Superintendent. He entered the service of the Company in 1872.

The membership of the New York Board of Directors is now (July 1898) as follows:

> Charles H. Marshall, Chairman,
> John A. Stewart,
> James E. Pulsford,
> John Crosby Brown,
> Edmund D. Randolph.

10

Of these, the Trustees of funds for the general benefit and protection of policyholders in the United States are:

>Charles H. Marshall,
>John A. Stewart,
>John Crosby Brown.

Mr. John A. Stewart, president of the United States Trust Company, joined the New York Board in February, 1881, and was thereupon made a Trustee.

Mr. John Crosby Brown, of Messrs. Brown Brothers & Company, was elected as Director and Trustee in January, 1890. His election brought to the Board once more a representative of the house which had taken so large an interest in the Company at its entry into this country, his father, the late James Brown, having for many years been Chairman of its first Board of Directors.

In November, 1890, Mr. Edmund D. Randolph, then president of the Continental National Bank, joined the New York Board. He is now chairman of the executive committee of the New York Life Insurance Company.

New York Directors.

John Crosby Brown.

John A. Stewart.

Charles H. Marshall.

James E. Pulsford.

Edmund D. Randolph.

Messrs. William F. Cary, Jr., Robert B. Minturn and Alexander Hamilton, Directors in New York, died during office.[1]   Mr. Anson Phelps Stokes resigned in December, 1889, in pursuance of an expressed determination to retire from all Directorships.

That the important services performed by all gentlemen holding the position on the Boards of the Company should receive the warm recognition of the Home Board and the stockholders as expressed at annual meetings on very many occasions, is surprising to none who have had the knowledge of the rare judgment with which important questions of investment or of general policy have been disposed of at all times in the history of the Company in the United States.

The membership of the Chicago Board as now constituted is as follows:[2]

> Ezra J. Warner, Chairman.
>
> L. Z. Leiter.

That of San Francisco:

> William Alvord, Chairman.

[1] Mr. Cary, died Sept. 9, 1880.   Mr. Minturn, died Dec. 15, 1889.
Mr. Hamilton, died Dec. 30, 1889.

[2] Mr. Henry W. King, died this year (1898).

William Babcock,

Levi Strauss,

Lovell White.

And that of New Orleans:

Gustaf R. Westfeldt, Chairman.

L. C. Fallon,

Lucas E. Moore,

C. M. Soria.

In referring, thus far, to the funds of the Company in the United States at various dates, and liabilities relating thereto, nothing has been said about the treatment of these assets and liabilities in order to arrive at the "capital" of the Company in the United States. Section 27 of the Insurance Laws of the State of New York provides that the capital of a company of a foreign country admitted to do business in that State after May 27th, 1880, shall not be less than $500,000 "deposited with Insurance Departments or held in trust by Trustees approved by the Superintendent of Insurance, and citizens of the United States, or deposited with a trust company to be approved by him, for the

CHICAGO DIRECTORS.

E. J. WARNER.

general benefit and security of all its policyholders
in the United States." The aggregate value of the
securities deposited in the prescribed way (the
securities being limited to such as fire insurance
companies of the State of New York may invest
their funds in) after deducting liabilities in New
York State and the other States of the United
States, constitutes the capital of the company. It
will be observed that the minimum capital of
$500,000 relates to companies of foreign countries
entering New York after May 27th, 1880. Companies admitted to transact business prior to that
date are required to have a capital of not less
than $200,000, such a sum being the minimum
capital required of fire insurance companies of
that State. Should the surplus, therefore, of the
foreign company entering New York prior to May
27th, 1880, appear to be less than $200,000, the
capital becomes under the law impaired, and this
impairment must be made good, the law so placing the foreign company in precisely the same
position as a company of the State.

The capital as so ascertained is subject to taxation exactly as is the capital of the native institution, and the foreign company may write, just as may the domestic company, ten per cent. of the amount on any one risk.

The capital of The Liverpool and London and Globe Insurance Company in the United States as ascertained in the prescribed manner was on December 31st, 1897, $2,895,757.80.

It would not have been strange if, in all these years—and during many of which the Company had been the subject of attack and criticism—a disposition on the part of State officials had been manifested to examine into its affairs, and yet with the exception of an inquiry of a cursory nature by the representative of a western State made at a time (1897) when no reasonable excuse existed for it, but one requisition was made on The Liverpool and London and Globe. In 1881 Superintendent Fairman of the Insurance Department of the State of New York, without questioning the correctness of the Company's sworn statement

San Francisco Directors.

William Alvord.

Levi Strauss.

William Babcock.

Lovell White.

of assets and liabilities, yet desired to know the character of loans on bond and mortgage, then amounting to $1,288,586. It was a reasonable inquiry, and was a welcome one to the Company. The appraisers selected by the Department to make the investigation concluded their report in the following words: "Finally in justice to the Company would like to say that with one or two exceptions we find their loans an extraordinarily good lot and excellently well secured."

Reference has been made in previous pages to the real estate of the Company in the United States. In New York City the site acquired is quite large, the frontage on William and Pine Streets being respectively sixty-eight and thirty feet. Evidences of a disposition on the part of the Company to make in other suitable places, as occasion offered, investments of like character were not wanting, and accordingly in 1883 a purchase was made in Philadelphia of the property at No. 331 to 337 Walnut Street. The old buildings standing on this site were torn down, and an attractive six-

story building was erected to supply the needs of
the Company at that point.   Again in 1884, the
office building owned by the Newark Savings Institution, at the corner of Broad and Mechanic Streets,
Newark, N. J., was purchased.   This subsequently
was considerably enlarged by the acquisition of
adjoining property, and the erection of a modern
office building on the site.   These, combined, furnish
a structure of considerable extent, the ground area
being no less than 11,000 square feet.

As to the purchase by the Company at New
Orleans, La., in 1894, it may be said that whether
in regard to desirability of location, durability of
structure, convenience in design, or attractiveness in
elevation, it has received wide commendation.   The
building embodies the ideas of the best minds
of the country in regard to fireproof construction
and electrical engineering, and is the latest, as it
is probably the finest, addition to the Company's
real estate investments in this country.

A complete list of the real estate assets as
reported at December 31st, 1897, is as follows: the

New Orleans Directors.

Gustaf R. Westfeldt.

C. M. Soria.

L E. Moore.

L. C. Fallon.

aggregate value on conservative estimates being
$1,745,000.[1]

> New York, 45, 47, 49 William Street; 41, 43
>   Pine Street,
> San Francisco, Cal., 422 California Street,
> Cincinnati, Ohio, corner Main and Third Streets,
> Charleston, S. C., 14 Broad Street,
> Richmond, Va., 1113 Main Street,
> Philadelphia, Pa., 331 to 337 Walnut Street,
> Newark, N. J., corner Broad and Mechanic
>   Streets,
> New Orleans, La., corner Carondelet and Com-
>   mon Streets.

Whilst in the aggregate this is not quite the
largest investment in real estate in the United
States by a fire insurance company, (it is second in
order) it is yet believed that, by its much wider distribution, it better accomplishes the purpose of the Company to place before the eyes of property owners (and
in the names of American citizens pledged to protect

1 The Montgomery, Ala., building was   The Richmond, Va., building was
sold in 1894.   bought in 1878.

their interests) these practical hostages for the
faithful performance of its contracts.

At the annual meeting of the stockholders of
the Company, held in Liverpool in May, 1895, a
well deserved compliment was paid by the General
Manager, Mr. Dove, to the agents in the United
States. Mr. Dove spoke as follows:

"The excellent returns received from every part
of the world showed in what manner their (the
agents') duties were carried out in the careful conduct of the Company's interests. He would like,
on this, the first occasion that they had ever had
one of their representative agents from America
present, to say how much they were indebted to
that large body of men, their agents, throughout
the world. In America they made a profession of
the insurance business, devoting their time and
energy to it. He wished to say that the work of
the Company's officers would all be thrown away
if it were not for the steady and careful work of that
large body of men, the agents, who used their
influence in getting business for The Liverpool

J. M. DE CAMP.

JAMES HENDRICK.

ATWOOD SMITH.

CHAS. E. GUILD.

and London and Globe and the other companies they represented, and who knew how to safeguard the Company's interests by taking account of the moral hazards all were trying to escape."

Mr. John Bibby, Chairman of the Home Board, speaking at the same meeting with reference to the presence on that occasion of Mr. John Crosby Brown, a Director on the New York Board, Mr. Lucas E. Moore, a member of the New Orleans Board, Mr. George L. Shepley, the Company's agent at Providence, R. I., and Mr. Henry W. Eaton, of New York, said:

"I feel that I may assure these gentlemen that they carry to their colleagues in America your most grateful thanks as shareholders in this Company for the untiring energy with which they have used their great influence in their respective centres in promoting your interests, both by the acquisition of good business and the successful investment of your funds."

❧   ❧   ❧   ❧

ð ð ð ð

The period covered by the operations of the Company in the United States is particularly interesting to the student of fire insurance history.

It begins with the advent of the foreign company, and by the gradual growth of feeling on the part of a large section of the insuring public in favor of the patronage of companies transacting a widely scattered business. Experience had already failed to justify the expectation that at a time of disaster, coming as the result of conflagration, the extraordinary claims naturally ensuing could be drawn from purely local sources.

President Charles J. Martin, of the Home Insurance Company, during an address made as early as 1863 [1] says:

"The New York fire insurance companies were twenty-five in number at the occurrence of the great (New York) fire in 1835, with stock capitals amount-

[1] *Fowler's History of Insurance.*

ing to little less than $8,000,000. This fire caused the insolvency of all but seven of such companies, and the capitals of these seven were impaired. Only about $1,000,000 of actual fire insurance capital was left. Insolvent companies paid from forty to ninety per cent. of the claims under their policies. To meet the deficiency in fire insurance capital, several mutuals were started. A part of these passed out of existence as old stock companies were revived, and the (New York) fire of 1845, swept away most of the remaining mutuals and caused the insolvency of several of the stock companies, and none of the latter were ever resuscitated."

An excuse for this reference is found in the assertion sometimes made, and most unjustly, that the foreign company is responsible for the decline of the small native institution. That the influence of competition is felt less in fire insurance than in other branches of business, cannot, it is true, be urged, but, as a distinct and satisfying cause, it can be said that the history of conflagrations furnishes all that is needful to explain the decline of the smaller institutions confining, or mainly confining, their operations to one locality.

From an examination of the *Spectator Chart* issued in 1898 it is seen that of the American stock companies established prior to 1848, thirty-six are in existence. So far as the disasters of 1871 and 1872 are concerned—and we may regard these as furnishing the most serious tests that could be applied of the resources of the companies—we cannot find that the survivors amongst the American companies doing a general business have suffered from a lack of patronage. On the contrary, after the Chicago conflagration to some extent, and in a much greater degree after the Boston conflagration, we see evidences of a marked growth of popularity in the great agency companies of the land.[1] And, apart from this, we find that, as a result of the experiences then gained, abundant proof of a disposition on the part of the stockholders of these institutions to practice self-denial

[1] There was, however, a rapid premium gain in companies which were showing ability to withstand the severest pressure of such conflagrations as those of Chicago and Boston.—FOWLER.

in the payment of dividends, to the end that reserves to meet serious emergencies could be accumulated. The most conservatively managed companies in the country operated in 1860 (the earliest year furnishing available departmental returns) on very small net surpluses, evidently relying upon cash capital to meet extraordinary claims.[1]

If the aggregate sum of risks in force of such of the thirty-six companies as reported in 1860 to the State of New York (thirteen companies) be compared with the aggregate sum reported at December 31st, 1897, it can be seen that it has increased eightfold. In the interval the aggregate net surplus has been increased over twelve million dollars.

If we turn to the records of the American companies established subsequent to 1848, and organized and maintained under principles, the adoption of which experience of the effect of conflagrations had shown to be a necessity, we can nowhere find that the advent of the foreign company has served

[1] Extract from New York Insurance Superintendent's report, 1873. " This sweeping conflagration (Chicago) should, and it is hoped will, act as a powerful instrument toward inducing the managers of companies to provide for the accumulation of large surplus of available assets beyond capital."

to operate to the disadvantage of the native institution. Of these companies established since 1848,
we have numerous examples of the acquirement of
a large business, accompanied by a success equal
to or greater than that which has attended the
operations in the United States of any foreign
company distinguished by good management, and
possessed of resources of a character to inspire the
confidence of the insuring public.

If, then, The Liverpool and London and Globe
and other companies of foreign countries have been
welcomed and honored here, so also, during the
same period of time, the Home, Continental, German-
American, Phenix, Glens Falls, Germania, Hanover,
and Niagara of New York, the Firemen's Fund of
California, the New Hampshire, the Springfield, and
the Phœnix, and National of Hartford, besides a
number of others, have been organized, and have
been operated on such lines that they have worked
side by side with the foreign companies under
conditions of competition admitting of material
progress, and, in many instances, of heavy gain.

The tendency of business, then, has been unquestionably towards the larger institutions. That any of the purely local companies should, in view of this tendency, survive and flourish at this date, would appear to be due to the exercise of remarkable ability and care on the part of those responsible for the conduct of their affairs.

During the period under review, the fire under-writer has been called upon to deal with new features or problems in the business such as never before, in any like period of time, have been presented to the profession for study and appropriate action.

Old methods of lighting by candle and vege-table or fish oil were to be largely eliminated on the discovery of mineral oil in considerable quantities in 1859, and suitable regulations for storage and use devised. The dangers of this product had to be carefully examined, and a concensus of opinion secured as to adequate charges for its use. At a

12

later period regulations became necessary when machines were invented for the manufacture of illuminating gas from naphtha.

The underwriter was invited to review his methods of rating, when, on the other hand, improved fire alarm and automatic sprinkler systems were forced upon his attention. It can be safely said that the stock company was unwilling in the early years of their introduction to offer practical encouragement to devices of an automatic character designed to extinguish fires, or to give prompt notice of their commencement.

The underwriter urged that, as an adjuster of rates, he was the creature of experience; that he had no material at hand to warrant him in making a discount to meet a problematical advantage, and he invited those who were concerned to reap the fruits of these inventions to give him the time needful to a proper observation of the effects so confidently claimed by the advocates of the apparatus. [1]

[1] The National Board, it is true, was induced in 1875 to devote, through its appropriate committee, some time to an inquiry into the first of these devices—the Parmelee—with the result that it was cordially commended to the "favorable consideration" of underwriters.

The attitude assumed by this interest drove the patentees into the arms of the "Mutuals," and then, and for many years afterwards, a large number of highly desirable risks equipped by the Parmelee Company passed from the books of the stock companies.

The "Mutuals," indeed, were in a proper position to test the merits of the invention, for, allowing nothing in advance for its introduction, the advantage, if any, to the policyholders could be reaped when at a later period dividends came to be distributed. [1]

The "Parmelee" gave way in 1882 to the "Grinnell," but not until 1886 did underwriters complete any organization for the purpose of

[1] That the Mutuals themselves were somewhat exercised when called upon at this time to deal with the subject is apparent from a most interesting paper recently published by Mr. Edward Atkinson, of Boston, and from which the following extracts are given.

"Having satisfied myself that the Parmelee automatic sprinkler was an effective safeguard, I secured the approval of the directors, and in 1880 undertook to bring it into general use. My coadjutors in other factory mutual companies, almost without exception, thought the effort would fail, while some of them were opposed to the undertaking. The first effort was to secure the introduction of the automatic system in all departments of textile mills in which the stock is worked in a loose condition, in opening, picking and spinning, and in other analogous departments in workshops and paper mills. We had not yet that feeling of positive assurance in putting sprinklers everywhere that would have warranted us in asking the very large expenditure since made in extending the service over weaving rooms and other departments. * * * * *

In the early history of this undertaking there was a grave doubt in my own mind, and in that of manufacturers themselves, as to the effectiveness of the service at certain points and in certain places, notably in the mule spinning room of a cotton factory.

regulating classes of business equipped with this or other approved device.

The credit for such action rests with the New England Exchange, an association of Special Agents, which after patient inquiry then, and since, arranged and perfected machinery for dealing with this important class.

The Phenix of Brooklyn first, with the Queen of England and National of Hartford, and followed somewhat later by The Liverpool and London and Globe, began to write largely increased lines on approved risks of this character, so laying the foundation for the establishment in 1890 of the Factory Insurance Association.

In the early eighties, underwriters were called upon to regulate the use of electricity utilized for heat, light and power; then the newly invented celluloid had to be studied and its risks estimated, and, in the recent past, acetylene has called for more than usual attention from underwriters, owing to the belief that, if storage and use be unguarded by stringent regulations, that product will furnish a loss experience which has been unprovided for in our existing systems of rating.

To secure co-operation on a comprehensive scale, the lack of which had been so often lamented, the National Board of Fire Underwriters was organized in July, 1866, and met with complete success. It was the first association of the kind in the history of fire insurance in the United States. It deserved and secured ample support; it formed a rallying ground for the companies after the disasters of 1871 and 1872, and remains to-day, after many trials, during which vexed subjects of discussion were eliminated, a strong and useful institution. Not the least of the results it attained was the adoption of uniform policy conditions, in which, amongst other features, the use and storage of mineral oils, gunpowder, etc., was suitably dealt with.

In changes in the organization and equipments of Fire Departments, by which in nearly all cities of any importance the volunteer system was eliminated, and manual engines superseded; in the gradual extension of approved methods of water supply and

distribution; in the introduction in very many of
the large cities of fire patrol organizations under
the control of the local underwriters; in the large
increase and great improvement in systems of
automatic sprinklers and fire alarms; in the invention and practical adoption of extinguishers for
ready use at incipient fires; in the large advance
in the methods of construction of fire-doors and
shutters; in the extended use of fire-proof material
in the erection of buildings; in the awakening of
governing powers to the need of more stringent laws
regulating the construction of buildings in cities, and
the proper storage of combustibles within their bor-
ders; in improved processes of manufacture by which
dangerous elements have been eliminated; in the
adoption of reasonable systems of rating (involving
the use of a co-insurance clause) by which one risk
can be measured with another and their relative
charges justified; in the organized examination of
risks by competent men, by which undesirable features
are removed and their fire equipment maintained in
a state of efficiency; in the co-operation by which

separation of merchandise in storage stores in large
cities—the fibre from the non-fibre—has been accomplished; in union for the purpose of securing and
maintaining rates of commission and brokerage at a
level deemed equitable as between the companies and
their agents; in the selection of men foremost in
the ranks of underwriters to form a tribunal for the
settlement of points in dispute between companies;
in the resistance organized to hostile and burden-
some laws of the State Legislatures; in the
establishment of a fund for the prosecution of
incendiaries; in the cultivation and undoubted growth
of a kindlier feeling between the companies; all these
and many more changes have been initiated during
the last fifty years, and have, each in its own appropriate way, been dealt with, and in them, and in
the councils of the companies wherein they were
entertained, The Liverpool and London and Globe
has borne its part.

And now we are about to take leave of the
story of the Company which, successively as the
Liverpool and London, and The Liverpool and

London and Globe, has been continuously before the American public for half a century.

Remembering that by the vocabularies "to insure" is "to make certain or sure; to make safe," effort has been made to give to this a liberal as well as a literal interpretation, to the end that the assured may "make certain" that in the hour of his trial he will receive the fullest measure of his loss within the bounds of his contract. Remembering, too, the old saying that "he gives twice who gives quickly," effort has been made to meet claims with promptitude, and with a generous recognition of the circumstances of difficulty and anxiety which misfortune has imposed on the assured. In respect to these endeavors, the Company may well entertain the hope that it has earned a place in the regard of the American people, and that, in the years to come, it may enjoy their respect and confidence.

That the Company will endure, none who have learnt its history, and are familiar with the spirit of its enterprise, can doubt. That it will continue to attract to itself that devotion from its representatives which has been so conspicuously exhibited during its entire career, can readily be believed. And if we pause to inquire in what manner the subject of this regard has assisted in influencing the success of which all connected with the Company may well be so proud, the answer is at hand.

It has given to its representatives an unstinted confidence: it has fortified its promise of safety to the public by a security which has never failed.

1848-1898.

13

Appendix

SPECIAL AGENTS.

To the special agents of all companies doing
a large agency business much responsibility attaches.
In the careful selection of men of standing in their
several communities to represent the companies as
local agents; in the constant watchfulness of the
character of business being written for the company;
in the personal surveys of remote and important
risks; in the prompt and liberal adjustment of all
honest losses; in their duties to local Boards and
State associations, and in the care at all times to
conserve and promote the mutual interests of the
company and its agents, the special agent is the
personal representative of the officers, and on his
success or failure depends in a great measure the

increase or decline of the Company's business in his field. He must continually be impressed with the importance of carrying out to its fullest extent the broad policy of the company to treat not only justly, but liberally, all who do business with it.

We recognize the fidelity with which our Special Agents serve the Company, and are sensible of the fact that their efforts contribute in no small degree to its prosperity in the field.

SPECIAL AGENTS.

G. A. FURNESS. Field, New England. Commenced duties as Special Agent in 1877, previous to which time he had been since 1873 in the New York office of the Company.

J. DE W. CHURCHILL. Field, the Virginias and Carolinas; has acted as Special Agent of the above territory since 1877. His insurance work commenced in 1853 as local agent at Toronto, Canada, for the Aetna of Hartford, Home of New York, and other companies. For some years subsequently was in the employ of the Aetna under J. B. Bennett, at Cincinnati, Ohio; later was with the National Board, and Secretary of the local Board at Buffalo, N. Y.

J. B. KREMER. Field, Pennsylvania, Maryland and Delaware; has supervised the above field as Special Agent of this Company since 1883. Entered the insurance business in 1872 as local agent at Philadelphia, subsequently did special work for the Scottish Commercial and the Lancashire.

C. F. HAWES. Field, New Jersey, southern New York and western Connecticut. Appointed Special Agent in 1891, previous to which time had been in the New York office since 1877.

C. E. WORTHAM, JR. Field, central and western New York. Appointed Special Agent in 1893. Prior to that year and with a brief intermission was indirectly in the service of the Company since 1878.

R. E. GOOCH. Field, Ohio. Entered the service of the Company in 1895, prior to which time he was in the employ of the Phœnix Insurance Company of England since 1886.

F. W. BAUER. Field, eastern New York, Vermont and western Massachusetts. Appointed Special Agent in 1896; previously in the New York office of the Company since 1879.

WM. B. SEAMAN. Entered employ of the Company in 1876. In 1884 was appointed Special Agent for western New York with headquarters at Rochester, and ten years later was recalled to New York to adjust losses for the Company in that city.

PRESTON T. KELSEY. Field, Indiana. Entered service of this Company 1897, previous to which he was for some time Special Agent of the Insurance Company of North America for Cook County, Ill., and later for the Hanover.

FRANK G. SNYDER. Field, Kentucky, Tennessee and Arkansas. Entered the Company's service in 1897, was Special Agent in the South in 1888 for the State Investment Company of California, and subsequently for the Orient; and later, for the Mechanics & Traders of New Orleans.

J. B. HEREFORD.   Field, Texas.   Embarked in local agency business at Dallas, Texas, in the year 1887, and in 1891 was appointed special agent of the Guardian Insurance Company of England, for the State of Texas, resigning that position in 1894 to accept the Special Agency of The Liverpool and London and Globe.

GUY CARPENTER.   Field, Alabama, Florida and Georgia. Entered the office of the Sun Mutual Insurance Company in March, 1885, and in June, 1892 accepted the position of fire clerk in the agency of Wm. M. Railey, where he remained until March, 1893, resigning to accept the position of Special Agent of The Liverpool and London and Globe Insurance Company.

E. H. ADDINGTON.   Field, Louisiana and Mississippi.   Entered a local agency in Portland, Ind., in the spring of 1882.   In December, 1886 came to New Orleans to serve as inspector of the compact under the management of the late J. B. Bennett, resigning after three years of service to accept the position of fire clerk with the Mechanics and Traders Insurance Company of New Orleans, La.   On January 1st, 1893, was appointed Special Agent of The Liverpool and London and Globe Insurance Company.

B. H. ABRAMS.   Field, Georgia, Florida and Alabama.   Has been Special Agent for these States since 1887, having resigned a similar position with the Capital City Insurance Company of Montgomery, Ala.   Was for several years previously a prominent local agent in Mobile, Ala.

14

CHAS. H. PESCAY. Field, Texas. Entered the office of S. O. Cotton & Bro., General Agents at Houston, Tex., in March, 1886, where he remained until March, 1892, resigning to accept the position of Special Agent of The Liverpool and London and Globe Insurance Company.

EDWARD G. SPROWL. Field, Oregon, Washington and Idaho. Has been in the employ of the Company in various capacities since 1871. Was appointed Special Agent in 1879.

R. G. BRUSH. Field, California, Nevada and Arizona. His insurance experience commenced in San Francisco in the early sixties, since which time he has been continuously in the fire insurance business in various positions. Was appointed Special Agent of this Company November 1st, 1891.

JOHN W. GUNN. Field, Oregon and Washington. Was appointed Local Agent in April, 1891 at Snohomish, Washington, and has been employed as Special Agent of this Company since October, 1897.

E. H. BERRY. State Agent for Wisconsin. Is now in his nineteenth year as field man for this Company, having commenced as Special Agent January 1st, 1880. In 1893 he was appointed State Agent for Wisconsin and upper Michigan, and since January, 1898, has been State Agent for Wisconsin alone, with headquarters at Milwaukee.

FREDERICK O'L BUCK. State Agent for Colorado, Montana, and Utah. Entered the insurance business in 1874 in Clearfield, Pa., and continued therein until 1877. In 1878 he went to Colorado and re-entered the insurance business at Georgetown. In 1887 he was appointed State Agent for this Company with headquarters at Denver, Colorado.

J. G. CARVER. State Agent for Michigan. Entered the insurance business in early life in connection with real estate and loaning. January, 1889, accepted a position with the First National Bank at Iron Mountain, Michigan, having charge of the insurance department until June, 1891, when he accepted the position of assistant to George H. Moore, State Agent of The Liverpool and London and Globe Insurance Company for Michigan, and succeeded him in this position January 1st, 1893.

WILLIAM E. HITCHCOCK. State Agent for Nebraska and South Dakota. Was a member of the firm of Webster, Howard & Company, one of the largest insurance and loan brokerage firms in the City of Omaha for many years. He entered this business some five years ago; became connected with this Company in 1897 as State Agent for Nebraska and South Dakota.

HUGH R. LOUDON. State Agent for Missouri. Entered the insurance business at an early age in the office of the Minneapolis Mutual Insurance Company of Minneapolis, and at seventeen entered the field for that Company. In 1891 was appointed local manager in Minneapolis and St. Paul for the Armstrong Mutuals of New York. Later was in the employ of the Lancashire until January 1st, 1894, when he became associated with this Company.

WILL S. LOUDON. State Agent for Iowa. Entered the insurance business at an early age with the Syndicate Insurance Company of Minneapolis in 1886, with which he remained for six years, filling during that time every office position. Later was connected with the Phenix of Brooklyn, and inspector for the Western Miller's Mutual in Wisconsin, Michigan, Indiana and Ohio. Subsequently he entered the local agency business in Minneapolis. Accepted his present position with The Liverpool and London and Globe Insurance Company in May, 1896.

JOHN E. THOMAS. State Agent for Illinois. Engaged in insurance business with his father under the firm name of J. V. & J. E. Thomas, and gradually assumed sole charge until January 1st, 1893, when the firm was dissolved. In 1894, he was appointed Special Agent of the Company for Northern Illinois, and one year later received his present appointment.

JOSEPH J. WINDLE. State Agent for Minnesota and North Dakota. Entered the insurance business at Madison, Wisconsin, in 1886 as local agent, but most of his time was devoted to adjustment work for different companies. He entered the employ of The Liverpool and London and Globe

Insurance Company in the beginning of 1889 as State Agent for Dakota Territory, and a few years later the State of Minnesota was added to his field.

EDWARD W. WINDLE. Special Agent, Minnesota and North Dakota. Commenced his business career in his father's office in England, where he received his early training in the insurance business. Later, he studied law for some years. He came to the United States in 1894, assisting his brother in the office until May, 1896, when he entered the service of The Liverpool and London and Globe Insurance Company in the position he now holds.

JOHN HANRAHAN. Special Agent for Cook County, Illinois. Entered the insurance business in the office of Moore & Janes, of Chicago, in April, 1883, since which time he has followed his chosen calling. Entered the service of The Liverpool and London and Globe Insurance Company in August, 1887.

M. W. VAN VALKENBURG. State Agent for Kansas, Oklahoma and Indian Territories. Purchased a local insurance agency in Topeka, Kansas, in 1887, in which The Liverpool and London and Globe Insurance Company was represented. In 1889 was appointed State Agent for this Company for Kansas and Missouri. His territory was changed in 1893 to Kansas, Oklahoma and Indian Territories, with headquarters at Topeka, Kansas.

It has been suggested that we recognize in the illustrations in this review those of our friends who have for a quarter of a century or more continuously represented the Company as agents, and we have pleasure in appending a list of such, giving names, locations, and dates of appointment. This list could be greatly enlarged did it include a record of agencies established more than twenty-five years. A careful inquiry shows that in very many cases the original firm name remains unchanged, although the present members have not yet attained the period of representation above referred to.

	Appointed
Robert C. Rathbone, New York City.	1856
Richard Mather, Ironton, Ohio.	1857
James Hendrick, Albany, N. Y.	1858
John C. Brockenbrough, Lafayette, Ind.	1860
David N. Kennedy, Clarksville, Tenn.	1860
C. B. Armstrong, Buffalo, N. Y.	1861
D. B. Stow, Rondout, N. Y.	1861
Atwood Smith, Philadelphia, Pa.	1865

JNO. C. BROCKENBROUGH.

R. C. RATHBONE.

RICHARD MATHER.

C. B. ARMSTRONG.

DAVID N. KENNEDY.

D. B. STOW.

O. M. EDWARDS.

WM. G. COYE.

M. J. FRANCISCO.

W. STEWART POLK.

W. H. HARDIN.

W. L. HOSKINS.

A. J. KAUFFMAN.

GEO. W. DEY.

P. J. OTEY.

J. M. JOHNSON.

FREDK. NASH.

V. SCHAEFFER.

Appointed

O. M. Edwards, Pittsburgh, Pa.	1866
William G. Coye, Hornellsville, N. Y.	1866
A. H. Crew, Chico, Cal.	1866
J. C. Duchow, Columbia, Cal.	1866
J. H. Pope, Colusa, Cal.	1866
Colton Greene, Memphis, Tenn.	1867
M. J. Francisco, Rutland, Vt.	1868
W. L. Hoskins, Owego, N. Y.	1868
W. Stewart Polk, Baltimore, Md.	1868
W. H. Hardin, Chester, S. C.	1868
Andrew J. Kauffman, Columbia, Pa.	1868
David A. Baum, San Francisco, Cal.	1868
George W. Dey, Norfolk, Va.	1869
W. R. Higby, Bridgeport, Conn.	1869
C. A. Hogan, Starkesville, Miss.	1869
A. T. Graves, Hazelhurst, Miss.	1869
J. C. Turner, Camilla, Ga.	1869
E. S. Drake, Port Gibson, Miss.	1869
P. J. Otey, Lynchburg, Va.	1870
J. M. Johnson, Marion, S. C.	1870
Valentine Schaeffer, Dayton, Ohio.	1870
Frederick Nash, Charlotte, N. C.	1870

15

	Appointed
W. N. Coleman, Reading, Pa.	1870
S. C. Lumbard, Ft. Wayne, Ind.	1870
B. R. Prince, Altaville, Cal.	1870
W. B. Davidson, Montgomery, Ala.	1870
P. M. Savery, Tupelo, Miss.	1870
T. W. Griffith, Newark, N. J.	1871
Gustav Frank, New York City.	1871
Chas. C. Terry, Hudson, N. Y.	1871
Jno. R. Hurley, Paterson, N. J.	1871
R. W. Woodward, Jersey City, N. J.	1871
T. B. De Forest, Bridgeport, Conn.	1871
Henry Bull, Jr., Newport, R. I.	1871
Jones Frankle, Haverhill, Mass.	1871
J. Allen Brown, Salisbury, N. C.	1871
L. S. Fish, Cleveland, O.	1871
J. W. Hinman, Clyde, N. Y.	1871
Charles W. Grant, San Francisco, Cal.	1871
Geo. Childs, San Francisco, Cal.	1871
William M. Dye, San Francisco, Cal.	1871
W. P. Coleman, Sacramento, Cal.	1871
Co. P. Reeves, Suisun, Cal.	1871
J. S. Hickok, Burlington, Vt.	1872

W. N. COLEMAN.

S. C. LUMBARD.

T. W. GRIFFITH.

GUSTAV FRANK.

CHAS. C. TERRY.

JNO. R. HURLEY.

R. W. WOODWARD.

HENRY BULL, JR.

JONES FRANKLE.

J. ALLEN BROWN.

L. S. FISH.

J. W. HINMAN.

JULIUS S. HICKOK.

C. W. HOWLAND.

W. D. NORTON.

W. E. CLARK.

I. C. HOWLAND.

WM. J. GREEN.

Appointed

Chas. W. Howland, Rockland, Mass.	1872
W. D. Norton, Phelps, N. Y.	1872
W. E. Clark, South Framingham, Mass.	1872
Chas. E. Guild, Boston, Mass.	1872
Isaac C. Howland, Abington, Mass.	1872
William Heeser, Mendocino, Cal.	1872
William J. Brodrick, Los Angeles, Cal.	1872
W. M. Weaver, Greensboro, Ga.	1872
W. G. Cain, Tyler, Texas.	1872
Wm. J. Green, Nyack, N. Y.	1873
Wm. C. Atwater, Derby, Conn.	1873
C. Willis Gould, Chelsea, Mass.	1873
J. A. Stover, Lansingburg, N. Y.	1873
Wm. E. Lincoln, Warren, Mass.	1873
A. Hoffman, Mt. Sterling, Ky.	1873
L. W. Puffer, Brockton, Mass.	1873
C. C. Burrill, Ellsworth, Me.	1873
J. M. Lockey, Leominster, Mass.	1873
N. Everett Silsbee, Lynn, Mass.	1873
J. A. Lineback, Salem, N. C.	1873
John Underhay, Holbrook, Mass.	1873
T. C. Collins, Middleboro, Mass.	1873

	Appointed
M. W. Farr, Augusta, Me.	1873
A. S. Service, Sharon, Pa.	1873
J. D. Davis, Corry, Pa.	1873
Thos. H. Spann, Indianapolis, Ind.	1873
John M. Spann, Indianapolis, Ind.	1873
Robert H. King, Lexington, Ky.	1873
J. Q. A. Williamson, Jersey City, N. J.	1873
Seelye Benedict, Brooklyn, N. Y.	1873
A. C. Monroe, Worcester, Mass.	1873
Wm. H. Brewster, Jr., Newburyport, Mass.	1873
Allen M. Brewster, Newburyport, Mass.	1873
William Vanderhurst, Salinas, Cal.	1873
L. N. Goldbeck, Austin, Texas.	1873
H. B. Kaulbach, La Grange, Texas.	1873

1848-1898.

WM. C. ATWATER.

C. WILLIS GOULD.

J. A. STOVER.

WM. E. LINCOLN.

A. HOFFMAN.

L. W. PUFFER.

C. C. BURRILL

J. M. LOCKEY.

N. E. SILSBEE.

J. A. LINEBACK.

JNO. UNDERHAY.

T. C. COLLINS.

J. D. DAVIS.

A. S. SERVICE.

M. W. FARR.

T. H. SPANN.

JNO. M. SPANN.

ROBT. H. KING.

MEMBERS OF THE COMPANY'S OFFICE STAFF OTHER
THAN THE EXECUTIVE, CONTINUOUSLY
IN THE SERVICE FOR OVER
TWENTY-FIVE YEARS.

New York Office:

    Edmund Tapscott, Railroad Department, October,
        1871.

    James H. Burnside, Risk Clerk, November, 1872.

    Frederick H. Vail, Cashier, January, 1873.

New Orleans Office:

    Jules T. Morel, Cashier, April, 1873.

Cincinnati Office:

    Walter Bryers, Bookkeeper, January, 1872.

STATEMENT OF ASSETS, LIABILITIES, AND SURPLUS OF THE UNITED STATES BRANCH, BEGINNING WITH THE YEAR 1880.

	Assets.	Liabilities.	Surplus.
1880	$4,462,065.00	$2,647,030.00	$1,815,035.00
1881	4,777,589.00	2,948,482.00	1,829,107.00
1882	5,212,937.00	2,759,847.00	2,453,090.00
1883	5,771,959.00	3,195,448.00	2,576,511.00
1884	5,941,474.00	3,360,480.00	2,580,994.00
1885	5,924.010.00	3,334,907.00	2,589,103.00
1886	6,639,780.00	3,686,553.00	2,953,227.00
1887	6,793,575.00	3,752,238.00	3,041,337.00
1888	6,963,811.00	3,963,284.00	3,000,527.00
1889	7,337,156.00	4,298,248.00	3,038,908.00
1890	7,459,995.00	4,453,861.00	3,006,134.00
1891	7,862,847.00	5,002,160.00	2,860,671.00
1892	8,193,023.00	5,163,827.00	3,029,196.00
1893	8,598,271.00	5,571,746.00	3,026,525.00
1894	8,498,268.00	5,427,079.00	3,071,189.00
1895	8,670,434.00	5,356,316.00	3,314,118.00
1896	9,339,545.00	5,246,085.00	4,093,460.00
1897	9,681,864.00	5,195,767.00	4,486,097.00

A. C. MUNROE.

SEELYE BENEDICT.

J.Q.A WILLIAMSON.

A.M. BREWSTER.

W. R. HIGBY.

WM.H. BREWSTER.

T.B.DE FOREST.

A.H. CREW.

J. C. DUCHOW.

C. W. Grant.

B. R. Prince.

J. H. Pope.

Geo. Childs.

Wm. M. Dye.

W. P. Coleman.

Wm. J. Brodrick.

Wm. Heeser.

Co. P. Reeves.

TABLE OF PREMIUMS IN THE UNITED STATES.

1848	$4,515.00
1849	7,900.00
1850	32,940.00
1855	380,292.00
1860	455,775.00
1865	1,122,897.00
1870	2,114,173.00
1875	2,328,139.00
1880	2,664,242.00
1885	3,553,506.00
1890	4,496,999.00
1895	5,600,129.00
1897	5,194,546.00

COMPANIES REINSURED.

Unity of England.	Philadelphia.
Pacific of California.	Fame.
Old Dominion of Virginia.	Franklin of New York.
Amazon of Cincinnati.	Guardian of New York.
Faneuil Hall of Boston.	Jersey City of New Jersey.

Standard of New York.

UNITED STATES BRANCH
ANNUAL STATEMENT.
December 31, 1897.

ASSETS.

Real Estate . . .	$1,745,000.00
Loans on Bond and Mortgage	3,674,371.14
United States 4% Bonds .	2,255,400.00
New York City 3½% Gold Bonds	107,500.00
City of Boston 5% Bonds	206,550.00
City of Richmond 8% Bonds .	6,800.00
Cash in Banks . . .	677,632.10
Uncollected Premiums . . .	940,141.95
All other Assets . .	68,469.03
	$9,681,864.22

LIABILITIES.

Unadjusted Losses	$556,098.00
Unearned Premiums .	3,889,687.28
Perpetual Policy Liability	325,150.73
All other Liabilities . .	424,831.16
SURPLUS . . .	**4,486,097.05**
	$9,681,864.22

WM. VANDERHURST.

C. A. HOGAN.

J. C. TURNER.

W. M. WEAVER.

L. N. GOLDBECK.

W. B. DAVIDSON.

P. M. SAVERY.

H. B. KAULBACH.

W. G. CAIN.

DAVID A. BAUM.

E. S. DRAKE.

A. T. GRAVES.

INDEX.

www.ingramcontent.com/pod-product-compliance
Lightning Source LLC
Chambersburg PA
CBHW020539270326
41927CB00006B/648